25 Biblical Sermon Outlines with Brisk Illustrations for

EXPOSITORY PREACHING

in Workbook Format

J. Michael Shannon

Robert C. Shannon

STANDARD PUBLISHING
Cincinnati, Ohio   3020

Dedicated to our wives,

who have suffered through our worst efforts
and encouraged our best efforts.

FOREWORD

What Is Expository Preaching?

In the long history of the church, every renewal of Christianity has been accompanied by a renewal of preaching. Each renewal of preaching has rediscovered Biblical preaching. Biblical preaching requires a commitment to learning and scholarship. "The Reformation grew out of university lectures. It was as he carried out his task of lecturing on the Bible—the Psalms, Romans, Galatians, Hebrews—that Luther made the theological discoveries that renewed the church and reordered its life" (C. K. Barrett, *Biblical Problems and Biblical Preaching:* Fortress Press, 1964, p.v.). "The prime movers in the nineteenth century effort in behalf of Christian unity and union, by a return to the Christianity of the Christ as it is described in the New Testament, were educated men" (B. B. Tyler, "Period of Organization, *The Reformation of the Nineteenth Century,* J. H. Garrison, ed., Christian Publishing, 1901).

The task of preaching today is difficult. The preacher is called upon to declare a message which is mighty enough to match the desperate plight of modern man. Such a message is not to be found in the treasures of human wisdom, but in the Bible. No word of advice or mere opinion rising out of the human scene can save us. The desperate needs of this age demand a return to strong, sound Biblical preaching. Through the ages, we have called it "expository preaching."

My good friend of many years, Robert Shannon, and his son, Michael, have written a book which calls us all to a kind of preaching which has proved its worth through the ages. They call us to have the courage to proclaim the message of the Bible. If the road is worn down with much traveling, it is so because it leads to a desirable destination. The Shannons challenge us to do "expository preaching." In dealing with this theme, I want to underscore two sig-

3

nificant aspects (both emphasized by the Shannons): that preaching must be solidly rooted in Scripture and that it must be directed to the needs of people today.

What Is Expository Preaching?

When you consult the older experts in homiletics—John Broadus, F. B. Meyer, Henry Burgess, Andrew W. Blackwood—you will find them not in precise agreement on what they mean by "expository preaching." Nearly all agree on the length of the passage handled (though Broadus says it may be "a very short" passage). Some stress the point of verse-by-verse, clause-by-clause treatment. This would seem to indicate that if the details of a passage were omitted from the sermon, it would not be expository. Others stress the didactic style and explanatory method as though the purpose of preaching was to explain a passage of Scripture.

We need a new definition of expository preaching. It is really too good a term to give up. We are going to seek a new definition in terms of substance rather than form. Biblical exposition needs to be limited only by the broad principle that the substance of one's preaching be drawn from the Bible. That means every sermon must be rooted solidly in Scripture. All true preaching, then, is expository preaching. The sermon may be based on the whole Bible, a book of the Bible, a chapter, a paragraph, a sentence, a phrase, a word, a character, a doctrine, a topic, etc. The one requirement is that the sermon be soundly and solidly rooted in the Scripture. That means concern must be shown for the literary–historical context, grammatical and lexical data, as well as the larger context of the entire book and the whole Bible. It means being a literate and devoted student of the Bible. This view has a large appreciation for the dedicated scholarship of the church.

Marvin R. Vincent, known to most of us for his *Word Studies in the New Testament,* wrote another book entitled *The Expositor in the Pulpit*. In that book he says, "the phrase 'Expository Preaching' properly covers *all* preaching. Exposition is exposing the truth contained in God's word: *laying it open; putting it forth* where the people may

4

get hold of it; and that also is preaching."

Donald G. Miller develops this workable definition of expository preaching:

"Expository preaching is an act wherein the living truth of some portion of Holy Scripture, understood in the light of solid exegetical and historical study and made a living reality to the preacher by the Holy Spirit, comes alive to the hearer as he is confronted by God in Christ through the Holy Spirit in judgment and redemption" *(The Way to Biblical Preaching,* Abingdon Press, 1957, p. 26).

There are three elements in this definition worthy of our attention: (1) Preaching is not merely a person speaking to other persons; it is an act. Preaching accomplishes something. As P. T. Forsyth said, "The Gospel is an act of God. Its preaching must therefore be an act, a 'function' of the great act. A true sermon is a real deed." A person is either made better or worse by the preaching of the gospel. Preaching never leaves a person where it finds him. Preaching must be based on the Bible. A message not based on Scripture may be called something, but it is not a sermon. (2) The substance of preaching, drawn from the Scriptures, is to be found by careful study in the light of the best methods of historical and exegetical research (God did address His revelation to our intelligence), but this process must be made alive by the Holy Spirit, who desires to speak now through the ancient witnesses. (3) The end of preaching is that the sermon should be transformed from a human conversation between preacher and people into a divine encounter between God and both preacher and people. Such a concept of expository preaching is according to substance (rooted in Scripture and applied to human needs) rather than form. We are free to use a variety of forms, but we may never violate the substance of preaching.

The Values of Expository Preaching

There are many values in Biblical preaching. First, you will always have a ready supply of preaching material. Recently I spent nearly three years preaching my way through the Gospel of Mark. It was one of the delights of my ministry. I am currently preaching through Ephesians, and in the second year am just beginning chapter four. I have hundreds of sermon ideas, more than I may ever be able to preach. If you preach through a Biblical book systematically, you will have an overabundance of sermon material. Second, Biblical preaching will give a breadth of scope to your preaching and a sense of balance and wholeness. It makes you study broad themes and deep currents. You will handle subjects that you would otherwise overlook or postpone. I preached five sermons on predestination as I worked my way through Ephesians. Often I have thought about predestination, but it seldom got into my preaching before I came squarely up against it in Ephesians. People today need the strength and vitality of the God who comes through the Biblical doctrine of predestination. Many feel the world is hopeless and meaningless. The Biblical concept of predestination will speak to that condition. The balance of God's sovereignty and man's free will is beautifully set forth in Scripture. Third, Biblical preaching will acquaint your people with the Bible and impart authority to your preaching. When R. W. Dale preached at Carrs Lane Church in Birmingham England, "the congregation was like one great Bible Class: there was a Bible open in almost every hand." When the Bible is used in the pulpit, the people have the best safeguard against error and the best of spiritual food for the soul. When one is a consistent expositor of Scripture, he finds that the message carries its own authority. People can never be saved by oratory and fervency, but they can be saved by hearing the Word of God.

A Proper Approach to Biblical Interpretation

As we study to preach Biblically, there are two dangers to be avoided: (1) The dogmatic approach, which uses Scripture as an arsenal or proof-texts to be arranged without regard to literary form, historical context, theological context, or even the best translation into English. Little attention is paid to the teaching of the passage or the book in which the isolated text appears. Such use cannot escape the charge of subjectivism, which twists the Scriptures to make them mean what the preacher wants them to mean.

(2) The impressionistic approach, which equates the message of the passage with any thoughts which fill the preacher's mind as he reads. It places Scripture at the mercy of human feelings and overlooks the historical context of the Bible. It is far too simplistic for any honest handling of the Scriptures. Today we know nothing better than the grammatical–historical approach to save us from the subjectivism that distorts Scripture. The preacher must be concerned with the text, grammar, historical context, and literary form of the passage as much as with trying to discern what the passage means today. The first responsibility is to discern what the passage meant to its original author. Only then may we ask what it means today.

Preach to the Needs of People

Another aspect of preaching needed today is that it must be related to the lives of people. One does not preach for the purpose of explaining a passage of Scripture. One preaches to bring men and women into contact with God so that their lives may be transformed. Much so-called expository preaching in the past has been deadly dull, uninteresting and irrelevant. Robert J. McCracken says, "The weakness of much expository preaching is twofold; it inclines to be tedious and colorless, and it is often detached and remote from the activities and concerns of everyday existence. Nobody will deny the industry and conviction back of it, but it lacks relevance and contemporaniety" *(The Making of the Sermon,* Harper and Row, 1956, pp. 36-37). As the sermon is prepared, there must ever be before us the faces of our people with their needs and our world with its tragic problems. The preacher must learn to apply Biblical insights to contemporary situations. An artist was sketching outdoors in the Barbizon District in France. He was working at his easel set up along a stream, when a group of four children appeared in front of him and watched every stroke of his pencil. Finally one said, "Mister, please get us in your picture!" That is the plea of every congregation as it faces the preacher on a Sunday morning, "Get us in your picture." Without that, there is no preaching. We need to have the eyes of Jesus—"When he saw he crowds, he had compassion for them, because they were harassed and help-less, like sheep without a shepherd" (Matthew 9:36). Somehow we must learn to feel the sense of insignificance felt by many in our world—the insecurity, the anxiety, the fear, the sense of emptiness, the feeling of futility and the absence of hope. The Bible speaks to every lonely condition of the human heart. It is the preacher's job to bring the sound message of Scripture and the crying needs of the human heart together. There can be no real communication of the gospel without participation in the life of our generation. T. S. Eliot once wrote, "To apprehend the point of intersection of the timeless with time, is an occupation for a saint." It is surely the occupation of the preacher. The fact is that in the preparation of a sermon, the sooner the preacher can involve the people who listen in the sermon, the better. There is a problem in nearly every pew, and the preacher must meet each one. Bring the sermon close to life.

There is always a need for more and better Biblical preaching. James Smart writes of "The Strange Silence of the Bible in the Church." Seminary professors have stories of preachers whose old sermons have been ruined by a course in sound Biblical exegesis. Many discerning church members know they get a lot of moralism and allegory in their preaching. We need more sound Biblical scholarship, and we need to see a closer relationship between Biblical studies and preaching. Edward Taylor's biting comment on one person's sermon might say something to some of us— "My dear brother, if your text had the smallpox, your sermon would never have caught it." The preacher must be a student (he dare not neglect his study), and he must be a student of Scripture. It is an arduous, life-long responsibility, but it bears joyous and rewarding fruit.

The Shannons have written a book which points in the right direction. Their book is intended to be suggestive, not exhaustive. They are encouraging us to root our preaching solidly in Scripture (note the helpful outlines of the larger chunks of Scripture) and to relate that preaching to the needs of people (look carefully at the abundance of helpful illustrative material). All that we have said about expository preaching is encouraged and set forward by their book.

They expect us to obtain the best volumes for study of Ephesians, Colossians, Philippians, and Philemon. Do careful exegesis. Find Paul's meanings for Paul's words. Be thoughtful as you make the long and perilous journey from the first century to the twentieth century, and seek to speak to the needs of today. Let the Biblical message come alive. Capture the fire of the Biblical message, cast it on the dry fagots of our own hearts, and let it burn. To learn to preach Biblically is one of the most thrilling and rewarding experiences a human being can know. It is the kind of preaching the church needs today. We thank the Shannons for beckoning us in the right direction.

> —Dr. Myron J. Taylor
> *Westwood Hills Christian Church*
> *Los Angeles, California*

CONTENTS

The Nature of Expository Preaching 13
How to Outline Expository Sermons 15
How to Use This Book 17

Sermons From Ephesians 19
  The Gospel Exalts Christ
    Chapter 1 20
  The Gospel Brings Change
    Chapter 2 24
  The Gospel Demands Proclamation
    Chapter 3 28
  The Gospel Issues a Challenge
    4:1-17 32
  The Gospel Makes Demands
    4:17-32 36
  The Gospel Offers a Model
    5:1-20 40
  The Gospel in the Home
    5:21—6:4 44
  The Gospel in the Church
    5:23-32 48
  The Gospel in Action
    6:10-20 52

Sermons From Colossians 57
  The Gospel We Believe
    1:6, 25, 26; 3:16 58
  The Savior We Worship
    1:13-27 62
  The Church We Serve
    1:24-29 66
  The Maturity We Seek
    2:2-7 70
  The Errors We Avoid
    2:8-31 74
  The New Life We Can Enjoy
    3:2-17 78

The Prayers We Offer
   4:1-4 82
The Partnership We Share
   4:5-18 86

Sermons From Philippians 91
   Live With Joy
      1:3-11 92
   Live With Perspective
      1:12-30 98
   Live With Humility
      2:1-12 102
   Live With Dedication
      2:12-30 106
   Live With Insight
      3:2-11 110
   Live in Determination
      3:12-21 114
   Live With Power
      4:1-13 118

A Sermon From Philemon 123
   Changes in the Lineup
      1-15 124

THE NATURE OF EXPOSITORY PREACHING

Expository preaching is preaching that draws its ideas from a passage of Scripture, usually several verses in length. The preacher limits himself to the ideas drawn from that text. He is not limited to the words of the passage and feels free to employ synonyms that suit his own style and purpose. He is not limited to the order of the text, but feels free to invert it or to arrange its ideas in any sequence that seems logical.

He is free also to treat the text in its widest possible form. He may, if he chooses, include the historical circumstances, the emotional state of the author, and the situation of the intended recipient. Nor must he confine himself to the central idea of the passage, though he must be aware of it. Its satellite ideas may be used. (Romans 6 is on the subject of sin, yet one may use the chapter to speak of baptism.)

The value of expository preaching is obvious. One is certain that he is preaching God's truth, not man's opinion. There is even more value in preaching through a book. Subjects come up naturally. No one can suspect that the minister is selecting his themes out of pique or whimsy.

If expository preaching has advantages, it also has dangers. It can degenerate into nothing more than a dull, verse by verse explanation. Bowie describes such preaching as "a few groping comments on each successive verse, like a blind man tapping with a cane." Paul S. Rees calls this "a caricature of expository preaching, without organization and without termination." It is, says Rees, "overweighted by technical and labored explanation and damagingly undernourished with such things as illustrations and applications." Expository preaching, then, ought to have an outline, illustrations, an introduction, an application, and a conclusion.

Two of these needs are addressed in this book: outline and illustration. It is expected that the preacher will make his own outline, using the one printed here as a starter and perhaps as a model, but modifying it to suit his own personality, his audience, and his aim. It is expected that he will select from the illustrations those that suit him and reject those that do not. Perhaps even those rejected can serve as a stimulus for finding better and more apt illustrations of his own. The object is to provide both a catalyst and a model.

The table of contents lists each sermon by topic. In some cases, the topic may also serve as a title. In other cases, a possible title is suggested on the outline page.

—Robert C. Shannon

HOW TO OUTLINE EXPOSITORY SERMONS

Asking a preacher where he gets his ideas for a sermon is a bit like asking a painter or a playwright where he gets his ideas. The making of a sermon is more art than science. Even an artist, though, will study and refine his technique. There is no process or procedure which can replace the mystery of creativity. However, having a plan can help discipline the mind, creating the right atmosphere for creativity. The following is a step-by-step procedure for developing an expository outline.

1. Read your chosen text in more than one translation.
2. Read commentaries on the passage.
3. Read sermons on the passage.
4. Reread the text, writing down the statements of fact or truth you see in the passage.
   Note: If you can diagram sentences, you could do that here. However, most find sentence diagraming too complicated and time consuming.
5. From your list of statements, find those which could be organized around a central theme and be well developed.
6. Make some of your statements more general and some more specific to suit your needs.
7. Write a one-sentence proposition which summarizes your entire message.
8. Settle on your final main points (there should be two, three, or four of these).
9. Write your points for alliteration, rhyme, or similar word combinations if it suits you. (Note: It is not wise to forsake the truth of a passage just to get a clever outline.)
10. Settle on your subpoints, using the same procedure as before; or simply ask who, what, why, and when.
11. Put your outline in final form.
12. Add illustrations.
13. Write out your message in full, if possible.

The most difficult part of the process is probably 4-7.

Let's illustrate how these statements of fact can suggest a sermon outline. We will illustrate on a shorter passage than we would normally use, but the process is the same.

If you were preaching from John 3:16, what statements of fact could you find in that verse? Your list could be as follows:

1. God loved the world.
2. God loved the world in a special way.
3. God sent His Son.
4. God sent His Son to save.
5. Whosoever believes in Him shall not perish.
6. Whosoever believes in Him shall have eternal life.

From this list, a three-point outline comes rather quickly:

I. The object of God's Love—the world
II. The character of God's love—He sent His Son
III. The goal of God's love—that the world should not perish

That outline is preachable. What is described briefly here, however, actually requires hard work and meditation. The Spirit blesses the preacher who is willing to pay the price. Remember the words of Paul Scherer, when he gave three secrets to better preaching. He said, "The first is hard work, the second is hard work, and the third is still more work."

—J. Michael Shannon

HOW TO USE THIS BOOK

It has been said that a written sermon is not really a sermon at all, but only the report of one. A sermon is an event! So an outline is not a sermon. It is a plan for one. It is not our purpose to present the whole plan, but to suggest a starting place for the preacher to make his own plan. This book is not intended to be a flight plan—only a compass pointing in a direction.

Many good preachers have difficulty finding a place to start in their sermon preparation. They waste time casting about in various directions. We suggest you begin by reading the text two or three times and making your own rough outline. Then look at ours. Does it emphasize the points you wanted to emphasize? Does it fit you? Does it fit the needs of your congregation?

It may be that you will want to make your own outline. There may be other times that you can modify our outline to suit your purpose. Is there something in the printed outline that should be omitted? Is there something that should be added? How can it be modified to suit your own style, congregation, and aim? Are there synonyms that better express the ideas of the text than the terms we've suggested? Look at the printed outline, asking yourself, "In what ways can this be improved?" Jot down your modifications right on the outline page—there is usually room for that. Extensive revisions can be made on a separate sheet.

Then read through the illustrations. Do not hesitate to use the ones that you can use. Discard the ones that you cannot use. However, do not discard them completely! File them away for a future day. Do our illustrations suggest other and better illustrations to you? Many television programs are "spin-offs" from existing programs. Are there "spinoffs" that come to you as you read the printed illustrations? Do they suggest sources you may explore to find your own illustrations? Do they suggest sources you may have overlooked? There is ample space between the illustrations for you to revise and add illustrations as necessary.

When you have gathered your materials, you are ready to

write. We suggest writing the sermon out in full. One 8½ x 11 page, typed single spaced, will provide five minutes of sermon. Not one man in a hundred can successfully preach from a manuscript; but writing it out helps to develop ideas fully and gives you confidence that you have prepared enough material.

From the written manuscript, make a key word list. This is all you need to take into the pulpit. Perhaps you may want to try memorizing the key word list and preaching the sermon without notes.

In any case, memorize word for word the introduction and conclusion. These will usually amount to only a few sentences. You should know exactly what you will say to begin and exactly what you will say to close.

Begin your sermon work on Monday. Work on it a little every day. That will give you confidence. Your mind will be saturated with the subject; and you will preach with power.

An important word about texts. Some of the texts in this book are very long. It would be a mistake to read such a long text at the beginning of the sermon. Sometimes you may want simply to summarize or paraphrase the text and read only significant verses. This is especially useful if the text is an entire chapter. Sometimes you may want to use a portion of the text as the Scripture reading earlier in the worship service. Sometimes you may want to divide the text and read a portion at each of several points in the sermon. Sometimes you may want only to allude to the larger portions of the text in a general way. In any case, to read an entire chapter at the outset of a sermon would be to lose the attention of the congregation.

Above all, approach your task with joy! There is no thrill greater than exploring an old text and finding a new thought, a new emphasis, a new application. That is the joy of preparing to preach. It is the joy of discovery. That is matched by the joy on Sunday morning when you can come enthusiastically before your congregation and say, "Look what I've found!"

—The authors

SERMONS FROM EPHESIANS

THE GOSPEL EXALTS CHRIST

"The Exalted Christ"

Ephesians 1

Introduction: The gospel exalts one, not many. It exalts Christ, not man. Our worship and life should also exalt Him.

Proposition: When we see the character and activity of Christ, we stand in awe before Him.

I. THE GRACE WE EXPERIENCE IN CHRIST, v. 2
   A. Abundant grace, v. 3
   B. Undeserved grace, vs. 4, 5
   C. Costly grace, v. 7

II. THE GIFTS WE RECEIVE FROM CHRIST, v. 11
   A. The gospel, v. 13
   B. The Holy Spirit, vs. 13, 17
   C. Eternal life, v. 18

III. THE GLORY WE SEE IN CHRIST, v. 18
   A. His victory, vs. 19, 20
   B. His authority, v. 21
   C. His priority, vs. 22, 23

Conclusion: Christ touches all of life, present and future, temporal and eternal, sacred and secular. But He touches no life without permission.

When Kaiser Wilhelm of Germany came to visit Jerusalem, they tore down part of the wall at the Jaffa Gate so that the Kaiser could enter without passing under an arch! Christ was a far, far mightier king, yet He stooped to enter this world through the tiny doorway of human birth!

Michael Hart has written a book entitled *The 100.* In it he lists by rank the most influential persons in history. He ranks Jesus as number three. Number one in his book is Muhammad, and number two is Isaac Newton. It would be interesting to know his reasoning. He says he puts Muhammad ahead of Christ because Muhammad was directly responsible for Islam and wrote the Muslim Bible, the Koran. Christ, on the other hand, wrote no book and had no direct personal influence on world events as Muhammad did. It is impossible for us to see that kind of reasoning. More books have been inspired by Christ and written about Christ than any other figure of history. He changed the world and men more than any other. Surely He ranks number one!

You see lots of interesting things on T-shirts. Some of them are funny, some are vulgar, some are insulting. One of the most surprising seen lately is this one with a verse from Romans, chapter eight: "We are more than conquerors through Him that loved us."

In 1722, Ole Lorenson experienced a storm at sea. He vowed that if he lived, he would make a significant contribution to the church. He did survive, and his contribution can be seen in the Folk Museum in Oslo, Norway. It is a lovely carved wood altar piece of the crucifixion. One panel shows the scene in the upper room. Another, the Garden of Gethsemane and the trial. At the very top of the altar piece is the resurrection. The guards lie prostrate. Jesus is coming forth from the tomb. The placing of the resurrection in the most prominent part of the carving was done deliberately. The most significant thing about Christ is His victorious resurrection.

Sir John Bowring was twice elected to Parliament. He spoke five languages at the age of sixteen. By the time of his death, he was said to be conversant in 200 languages. He was knighted by the queen. He was governor of Hong Kong. He wrote thirty-six books ranging from religion to politics. Yet all that is current from his pen is a poem he wrote. A poem set to music. A poem that has become a hymn. He wrote it as he sailed along the China Coast. He passed Macao, where an earthquake had leveled the city. He saw the ruins of a mission church. The cross which had stood atop the chapel now stuck out of the ruins. Musing on that, Bowring wrote these lasting words:

> In the cross of Christ I glory
> Tow'ring o'er the wrecks of time

Everybody is familiar with Murphy's Law. "If anything can go wrong, it will." That has spawned a whole set of such tongue-in-cheek "laws." One of them is O'Reilly's Law of the Kitchen: "Cleanliness is next to impossible." We've all heard that "Cleanliness is next to godliness," but don't you sometimes feel that cleanliness is next to impossible? Spiritual cleanliness is only possible by the grace of God through Christ. Without Christ, it is impossible. We need abundant grace.

THE GOSPEL BRINGS CHANGE

"There'll Be Some Changes Made"

Ephesians 2

Introduction: A once popular song speaks of changes in life, changes in the weather, changes in self.

Proposition: When someone accepts the gospel, he cannot remain the same; inevitable changes become a part of his life.

I. A CHANGE OF ALLEGIANCE, vs. 1-3
  A. We must abandon the ways of this world.
  B. We must abandon the ruler of this world.
  C. We must abandon the desires of this world.

II. A CHANGE OF POSITION, vs. 4-13
  A. We have been raised by Christ, v. 5
  B. We have been seated by Christ, v. 6
  C. We have been brought near to God, v. 13

III. A CHANGE IN CONDITION, vs. 14-22
  A. Enemy to friend, vs. 14, 15
  B. Divided to united, v. 16
  C. Alien to citizen, v. 19
  D. Orphan to child, v. 19

Conclusion: The once desolate house is inhabited by God. vs. 20-22

Doctors and preachers are alike. Whatever is wrong with you, the doctor says it's a virus; the preacher says it's sin! But there *are* many, many viruses that plague us; and sin really is the cause of our problems. Sometimes sin is an indirect cause, sometimes a direct cause; but sin does cause our problems.

Gaston Bachelard wrote: "If one were to give an account of all the doors one has closed and opened, of all the doors he would like to re-open, one would have to tell the story of one's entire life."

James Morris said that England's Oxford University "was a sad reminder of what the world might be." The life of Jesus is a sad reminder of what we might be—but it is also a happy reminder of what we can become! Norman Rockwell said, "I paint the world as I would like it to be." In Jesus, we see ourselves as God would like us to be—and as His grace can make us to be!

Most religious bumper stickers leave us cold; but this one makes a point: "The Force Is With Me . . . His Name Is Jesus." Indeed, what a powerful force Jesus is. We see it in the world; and we see it in ourselves. In the largest dimensions and the smallest dimensions. His power to change is evident.

There was a young convert in Haiti whose family believed in voodoo. They urged him not to forsake the family faith for this new Christian religion. But he ignored the family pressures and came for baptism. He walked into the water, stopped, and turned back! The missionaries were sure he had changed his mind. They were certain that the family pressures had prevailed. But he went back to shore to empty his pockets of all his voodoo charms. Then he re-entered the stream and was baptized.

In Birmingham, England, there is a group of institutions of higher learning that are grouped together as the Selly Oak Colleges. One is called Crowther Hall. It is named for Samuel Crowther, who began his life as a slave in Africa and ended his life as a bishop of the Anglican church. We all began as slaves—slaves to sin. We end our lives as priests and princes. "He hath made us kings and priests," says Revelation, chapter 1.

When the same royal family ruled both Spain and France, it was said, "There are no more Pyrenees." For centuries, those high mountains had divided the two nations, and now they were politically united, even if they were geographically separated. But the mountains were still there, and the union did not last. When we come to Christ, all barriers that divide us are no more.

A recent political cartoon showed two people talking in an animated way. One said, "You wouldn't believe what I heard about Nancy Reagan!"

The other responded, "I believe! I believe!"

We are so quick to believe the ugly, so slow to respond to the lovely. We are so quick to believe gossip, so slow to believe gospel. We are so quick to believe slander, so slow to believe Scripture.

THE GOSPEL DEMANDS PROCLAMATION

"News Too Good to Keep"

Ephesians 3

Introduction: When we receive really good news that affects us personally, we cannot keep quiet about it. The gospel is this kind of news, for it is about Christ and His blessings.

Proposition: When someone really understands the implications and urgency of the gospel, he can't help but share it.

I. A MYSTERY TO BE REVEALED
   A. A truth, vs. 1, 2
   B. A revealed truth, vs. 3, 5
   C. A welcome truth, v. 6

II. A COMMISSION TO BE OBEYED
   A. A divine Commander, v. 7
   B. A humble servant, v. 8
   C. An eternal purpose, v. 11

III. A BLESSING TO BE IMPARTED
   A. The blessing of support, v. 16
   B. The blessing of presence, v. 17
   C. The blessing of insight, vs. 18, 19

Conclusion: We should spread the gospel because it is both a responsibility and a privilege.

Someone said, "You cannot see God's face and live." An old saint said, "Then let me see God's face and die!" In Scripture, God has revealed himself to us. He has not revealed His face but something more important than that. He has revealed His character—and His love.

In Kenya, Africa, among the Masai, is a Christian named Kimiti Ole Rerente. He has never been to school, but he has memorized great portions of Scripture. He preaches the gospel in neighboring villages. He teaches children. He has won his whole family to Christ. He assists the missionaries in their tasks. He is a Christian who has truly found the good news too good to keep. Oh, one more thing: he is blind!

It is almost impossible for anyone to see a rainbow and not point it out to someone else. Did you ever notice that? It's the kind of thing that just must be shared. You see one, and you want to tell someone about it at once. If you have ever been by yourself and seen a rainbow, you probably found it frustrating. There was no one to whom you could say, "Look! See the rainbow!" The gospel is such a beautiful expression of God's love that it just must be shared.

There are two kinds of books that always sell well—mysteries and love stories. The gospel is both. It is a mystery, long hidden, at last revealed. It is a love story in the finest sense of that word, for it unveils God's love for the world and for us.

Islam, the religion of the Moslems, is built about a stone that is said to have come down from Heaven. It is kept in a very sacred building, the Kaabala, in a very sacred city, Mecca, where no non-Moslem is allowed to go. We believe it was not a stone that came down from Heaven, but a message, a word, a gospel!

Letters are ended with a phrase that English teachers call a complimentary close. Nowadays, it's usually one word, like "Cordially" or "Sincerely" or "Fondly." It used to be that such letters always closed with, "Yours truly," and before that the odd phrase, "Your obedient servant." That's the way our prayers should close! That should characterize our attitude to God: "Your obedient servant!"

THE GOSPEL ISSUES A CHALLENGE

"I Dare You"

Ephesians 4:1-16

Introduction: The gospel calls for our best. God is not afraid to challenge us.

Proposition: The church and the individual must respond to God's challenge.

  I. RETAIN UNITY, vs. 3-6
    A. One body
    B. One Spirit
    C. One hope
    D. One Lord
    E. One faith
    F. One baptism
    G. One God

 II. RECOGNIZE DIVERSITY, vs. 7-12
    A. Each gift is given by Christ.
    B. Each gift enriches the church.

III. REACH MATURITY, vs. 13-16
    A. We must no longer be spiritual infants.
    B. We must strive to grow.
    C. Our goal is to measure up to Christ. We keep working on that through life. Though we never quite achieve it here, we may achieve it hereafter in Heaven.

Conclusion: Let us never be content, but keep on growing. Let us also provide a climate in which others can grow. Let us encourage them.

Every tool in the carpenter's box has its purpose. No one can do without the others. It might be argued that the plane has no depth, the hammer is too loud, the sand paper is too rough, the knife is too sharp, the screwdriver is too pointed. However, each is necessary; and each is fitted for the particular task that needs to be done. One tool cannot despise another! Of course, we are more than tools; but the lesson is obvious. God did not mean for us all to do the same thing. What each one does is very important and enables the other to do what he is equipped to do.

It is important to remember that Jesus did not quit meeting with His disciples because Judas was a traitor and a thief, because Peter was fickle, or because Thomas had his doubts. His disciples were at times rude, thoughtless, unkind, and selfish. His disciples still sometimes manifest those attitudes. But He does not forsake them; nor should we forsake them. Rather, we are to encourage the best and overlook and forgive the rest. In this way, we can create a climate for growth, all the while being thankful that people have been patient with us as well.

A worried father asked the doctor why his baby had not laughed. The doctor explained that a baby does not ordinarily laugh until the age of four weeks. "At that time," he said to the father, "the baby can see you clearly!"

The Fuller brush is famous. It all began with a shy, twenty-year-old man who had not done well in school. He lost the first three jobs he had and could not find another. In desperation, he began to make brushes. Then he started selling them, door to door. He did pretty well. He found that there were things he could do well, and he did them.

Two brothers in Scotland fell into an argument over the division of their father's estate. They came before a very wise judge who settled it this way: "Let one brother divide the estate into two parts, and let the other brother pick which part he wants!" Money is only one of the things that divides brothers. Even Christian brothers sometimes divide; but it is rarely over anything important. Sometimes it is over power, or prestige, or popularity, or personality. Christ has a solution even better than that of the Scottish judge. Paul expresses it when he says, "Let each esteem the other better than himself."

The seven sides of unity in Ephesians 4 are not the units of unity. The units of unity are individuals, but these are the facets of unity. As a diamond has many faces, so the lovely jewel of Christianity has many dimensions. Each dimension is important. No dimension may be safely ignored. Only when all seven faces are shining brightly does unity sparkle with radiant beauty.

We used to speak of "growing pains." Growing up is indeed a painful process, as any adolescent knows—and as any parent of an adolescent knows! Growing up spiritually is painful, too. It takes time. We are foolish to expect instant maturity on the part of Christians. We are equally foolish if we are content with stunted growth and arrested development. Somewhere in between those two extremes we must stand: encouraging growth and development, yet not expecting instant maturity.

THE GOSPEL MAKES DEMANDS

"The Power of Negative Thinking"

Ephesians 4:17-32

Introduction: We have all heard of the power of positive thinking, but Paul also speaks of the power of negative thinking. However, we most appreciate the demands of the gospel if they are put in the form of positive directions.

Proposition: Christianity makes moral demands.

I. THINK RIGHT, vs. 17-24
   A. Not as the godless
   B. Not as the hardhearted
   C. Not as the ignorant

II. TALK RIGHT, vs. 25-29
   A. No lying words
   B. No angry words
   C. No insincere words
   D. No unwholesome words

III. ACT RIGHT, vs. 30-32
   A. Be careful.
   B. Be courteous.
   C. Be kind.
   D. Be compassionate.

Conclusion: We speak of a well-rounded personality; but there are three sides to character, and each part is necessary if one is to be a whole person and a holy person.

In New Zealand, they have a saying, "She'll be right, mate." Whenever anything is worrisome or anything goes wrong, you will hear that optimistic sentence. "She'll be right, mate." That is certainly a good and helpful way to look at life. There is value in positive thinking. There is also value in negative thinking. There are some things that will not be right until we put them right. There are some things that will not be right until God puts them right.

In Edna St. Vincent Millay's poem, "Concert," there is a verse spoken by a girl as she leaves her lover to attend the symphony alone:

"Come now, be content.
I will come back again to you:
    I swear I will.
And you will know me still.
I shall only be a little taller
    Than when I went."

After we have been in the presence of Christ, we are always a little taller than when we went!

H. G. Wells once said, "If there is no God, nothing matters. If there is a God, nothing else matters!" That ought to highlight our need to walk in God's ways, to talk in a fashion that pleases Him, and to think on those things that honor Him.

Do you remember the chant from childhood: "Sticks and stones may break my bones, but words will never hurt me." It isn't so. Every one of us has sometimes been hurt by words. We have been hurt by lying words. We have been hurt by unkind words. We have been hurt by angry words. It is our place to forgive and forget—but also to be instructed by such experiences so that our words do not bring pain to others as others' words have brought pain to us.

Everyone is familiar with that splendid organization, Alcoholics Anonymous. The idea has worked so well that it spawned Gamblers Anonymous and Overeaters Anonymous. Now, there is a new one. It's called Anonymous Anonymous. It is for all the people who do not want anybody to know what their problem is. We know the problem, however. It is sin. The old man must be crucified and buried and his deeds buried with him.

When we "get even" with someone, that is exactly what we are doing. We are descending to their level. Instead of walking on a higher plane, we are stooping to the same low level they occupy.

Recently, United Press International reported on the large number of Christian converts in the world of music. Bonnie Bramlett, Bob Dylan, Donna Summer, B. J. Thomas, Richie Furie, and Al Green are among them. They all achieved success in the world of entertainment, but found life empty without Christ. All people need to experience the new life and walk the new ways of Christ. For that there is no substitute—not fame, not money, not success, not anything!

Viola Tyrrell writes about Omnephris, a young man who lived in A.D. 60. Madly in love, he hired a trumpeter to walk before him and a crier to walk behind him. As he paraded through the streets, the crier shouted, "The noble Omnephris doth love the beautiful Dionysia." Dionysia relented and married him, saying, "How can I doubt the love of him who hath trumpeted me abroad?" How can we doubt God's love when He offers us such newness? Does God have reason to doubt our love? Are we too coy and shy in showing that we love God and all His children?

THE GOSPEL OFFERS A MODEL

"A Career in Modeling"

Ephesians 5:1-20

Introduction: There are many ways to learn, but we learn best by imitation.

Proposition: God offers us, through Christ, an example to follow.

I. WALK IN HIS LOVE, vs. 1-6
   A. Some sins show we do not love others.
   B. Some sins show we do not love ourselves.
   C. Some sins show we do not love God.

II. WALK IN HIS LIGHT, vs. 7-14
   A. Fruitful in life
   B. Open to the world
   C. Pleasing to God

III. WALK IN HIS WISDOM, vs. 15-20
   A. Wise in the use of time
   B. Wise in conduct
   C. Wise in the will of the Lord
   D. Wise in worship

Conclusion: God has not left us to our own devices. We are compelled to exchange our ideas for His ideas.

Light purifies! Who has not heard of the ultraviolet ray? Light makes growth (and life itself) possible. Who has not heard of photosynthesis? Light makes it possible to move about safely. Light enables you to find your way. Light provides protection. Light makes it possible to read and learn. Light gains our attention. Light points the way. Now, with the laser beam, light heals. How very much is involved in walking in the light!

The well driller found water at ninety-five feet but insisted that he ought to drill deeper. It was not enough water. He found water again at 120 feet. There was plenty of it, but it was not pure enough. He drilled deeper still till there was abundant water and pure water. Are our lives too shallow? Do we suffer from a lack of spiritual reserves? And are we accepting the impure rather than going down deeper to the pure?

Have you heard the expression, "His life is an open book"? Since "all things are open" to God, we ought to live our lives without the need for secrecy. In our day, some have taken that to the other extreme. They have insisted that every random thought and every fleeting feeling must be trumpeted to the world. No, we are entitled to some inner privacy. The anger we feel today may be gone tomorrow. The doubt that assails us in the morning may vanish by noon. We need not advertise our every thought or deed. But we ought to live so that we need never hide our thoughts and deeds.

Because her last name is Wise, she collects owls. You will find them all over her house, and often she wears an owl on her clothing. Do you suppose that it puts an extra burden on a person to have the last name Wise? In Virginia, there is a city named Wise. Would you feel it a responsibility to live more wisely if you lived in Wise, Virginia? Probably, most people never give a thought to the name of the town or the name of the family. But every one of us needs to be wise, not in worldly wisdom, but in that wisdom that comes down from above.

A little boy had difficulty pronouncing some words. The word *worship* was one of them. He said, "We go to church to wash up." Notice that to Paul, worship and ethics were bound together. He speaks of them in the same breath. He writes of them in the same paragraph, almost in the same sentence. We like to separate them, but our religion will not allow that. Sinful living impedes worship. Sincere worship improves lives. No one should stay away from worship because he has sinned, but everyone should recognize that what we do in church on Sunday and what we do at work on Monday are not separate.

A model must be a perfect size something. It matters little what size; but the model must fit the size perfectly. Some of us are one size on top and another size on the bottom. Christ is our model. Life as it ought to be lived fit Him perfectly. Does it not sometimes seem that our Christianity is two sizes too small, that it pinches and constricts us? Or does it seem that it is sometimes a size too large, all baggy and wrinkled? Let's not alter the garment! Let's alter ourselves.

THE GOSPEL IN THE HOME

"Three Keys to a Healthy Family"

Ephesians 5:21—6:4

Introduction: The Bible is the most practical book on earth. It gives us sound advice for everyday living. Especially helpful is the advice given to families.

Proposition: The Bible has an ideal for the family that is practical and attainable.

I. CARE FOR EACH OTHER, 5:25-29; 6:1-3
   A. Husband and wife relationship
   B. Parent and child relationship

II. SHARE WITH EACH OTHER, 5:29-31
   A. A merging
   B. A miracle
   C. A mystery

III. BEAR WITH EACH OTHER, 5:21, 22; 6:4
   A. Cooperative submission
   B. Mutual submission
   C. Willing submission

Conclusion: God cares what happens to our earthly families, but whatever the situation with your earthly family, you have a heavenly family in the church.

A researcher at the University of Wisconsin, Mary Ann Fitzpatrick, says that nearly half the married men in America are "emotionally divorced" from their wives. We take that to mean that they are living together but not sharing emotionally, not showing care and concern. The solution is not for the emotionally divorced to get legally divorced. The solution is for them to be emotionally remarried to their wives. Christ loved the church, declared His love, and demonstrated His love. If men are to love their wives as Christ loved the church, they must say so and then show it by their deeds.

In Dick Browne's "Hi and Lois" comic strip, the next-door neighbor says, "Irma and I have been fighting a lot lately. I've been thinking about looking into a 'no fault' divorce." Hi answers, "What this country needs is more 'no fault' marriages."

James Thurber wrote: "Marriage is so much more interesting than divorce. It's the only time an immovable object successfully meets an irresistible force!"

A wife went to the police station with her next-door neighbor to report that her husband was missing. The policeman asked for a description. She said, "He's 45 years old, 6 foot 3, has blue eyes, blond hair, an athletic build, weighs 185 pounds, is soft-spoken, and is good to the children." The next-door neighbor protested, "Your husband is 5 foot 3, chubby, bald, has a big mouth, and is mean to your children." The wife replied, "Who wants *him* back?"

David Reuben wrote: "A marriage is like a long trip in a rowboat. If one passenger starts to rock the boat, the other one has to steady it. Otherwise, they will both go to the bottom together." How well that illustrates the mutual responsibilities and mutual concerns that must be a part of marriage.

The *New York Times* reported on a Wisconsin study of divorced couples with children. It revealed that 52% of them were back in court within two years of their divorce. The majority of them reappeared in court from two to ten times; and one father had a total of seventy-six court appearances in two years!

A five-year study by Mavis Hetherington of the University of Virginia concluded that the worst victims of divorces are small boys. And regardless of gender, children of divorced parents cause a disproportionate share of problems in schools. They do worse academically. If present trends continue, 48% of the children attending school in the 1990's will be from broken homes. Problems are ahead. They are problems that can be prevented far easier than they can be solved.

Redbook magazine recently reported that money and in-laws are no longer the major causes of divorce, though they once were. A new study shows that lack of communication, changing goals, and sexual problems are the major causes of marital difficulties. Whatever the causes, we know the cure. If we care for one another and share with one another and bear with one another, we can spare ourselves many heartaches and spare others much pain.

THE GOSPEL IN THE CHURCH

"Christ's Dearest Love"

Ephesians 5:23-32

Introduction: In a day when many deny the importance of the church, we do well to remember what Paul said about the church.

Proposition: The church is too precious to God to be taken lightly by men.

I. THE CHURCH IS SUBJECT TO CHRIST, v. 23
   A. He is the head.
   B. He is the Savior.
   C. He is the bridegroom.

II. THE CHURCH IS SEPARATED FROM THE WORLD, vs. 25-27
   A. The Means: by washing of water by the Word
   B. The Purpose: to show His glory
   C. The Culmination: to present her to himself

III. THE CHURCH IS SURROUNDED BY LOVE
   A. Christ cherishes the church, v. 29.
   B. Christ nourishes the church, v. 29.
   C. Christ died for the church, v. 25.

Conclusion: Our greatest privilege is to be part of Christ's great love: the church.

The fifty-cent U.S. postage stamp bears a picture of Lucy Stone, an early feminist who refused to wear her husband's name when they were married, but continued to use her maiden name. Perhaps that is not too important. Names serve only for convenience. What is important is that both partners in a marriage see themselves willingly and lovingly and mutually submissive to one another. And in the church, we must see ourselves equally submissive to Christ.

What is more treasured than the family picture album? A couple whose house burned down named that as their greatest loss. The material things could be replaced; but the loss of treasured family pictures was very painful. In the family picture album, the most treasured pictures are those of the babies; but after that, those of the brides. The Bible gives us a lovely picture of the church as the bride of Christ.

A minister was visiting in London. The guide showed him through Westminster Abbey, where so many of the nation's renowned are entombed. The guide said, "England's great sleep within these walls." The minister murmured, "I feel right at home." We must be alert in worship, and we must be alert in service. The church is set apart for a holy purpose and must be awake to both the responsibilities and the opportunities of the hour.

In England, the first church buildings were built on the sites of pagan temples and were sometimes the only public land. So people came there to buy and sell, for sports, and for public meetings. The church is, indeed, interested in the whole man and in the whole of life. However, the church is set apart for spiritual purposes. We speak not of the building, but of the church itself as a spiritual entity. The church has a holy purpose that must not be forgotten.

Many times we have heard it said that the church is surrounded by an evil and hostile world, like a besieged fortress. We need to remember that it is also true that the church is surrounded by God's love and care! Individually and collectively, we are blanketed by God's love as the earth is blanketed by the atmosphere. God loves the church and will never forsake her.

The Spaniards who conquered South America destroyed the Aztec temples because they were the place of human sacrifice. The Germans, in an earlier age, built their churches upon the ruins of Roman pagan temples. So, in a sense that goes beyond land or buildings, the church rises above the ruins of paganism and idolatry. Designed by God, empowered by the Spirit, loved by Christ, and served by Christians, the church must always stand taller than any other human achievement.

In one Southern city, three churches stood, each a block apart from the other. One built a new building with a tall steeple. The next built a new building with a taller spire. The third built with a still higher steeple. People in town called it "the steeplechase." We must strive to rise high, not architecturally, but spiritually. We must rise above the world and its sins. We must rise above our own pride and vanity, above our own weaknesses, doubts, and fears.

THE GOSPEL IN ACTION

"On the Front Line"

Ephesians 6:10-20

Introduction: We all want to be where the action is. Paul saw the action in a spiritual conflict between good and evil.
Proposition: The strength we receive from the gospel translates itself into everyday experience.

I. OUR CONFLICT, vs. 10-12
  A. Against the devil
  B. Against principalities and powers
  C. Against rulers of this world
  D. Against wickedness in high places
  E. Not against flesh and blood

II. OUR CLOTHING, vs. 13-17
  A. The armor
    1. Truth
    2. Righteousness
    3. Peace
    4. Salvation
  B. The weapons
    1. Faith
    2. The Word of God

III. OUR CONCERN, v. 18
  A. Concerned at all times
  B. Concerned for all Christians
  C. Concerned with all perseverance
  D. Concerned in all prayers

IV. OUR CONFIDENCE, vs. 19, 20
  A. Speak boldly
  B. Speak authoritatively
  C. Speak properly

Conclusion: We have not been placed in the world unprepared. God has provided the protection and power we need.

"There is a tide in the affairs of men, which, taken at the flood, leads on to fortune; omitted, all the voyage of their life is bound in shallows and miseries. On such a full sea are we now afloat; and we must take the current when it serves, or lose our venture."—Shakespeare.

Gordon McLaughlin is a native New Zealander. That gives him the right to speak of his own nation. He has written a book about his homeland entitled *The Passionless People*. He calls modern New Zealand "a sterile society." Could that be said of some congregations? Are we a passionless people? Or are we caught up in the grand passion Christ shares with His servants, to redeem the world?

Cato ended every speech he gave in the Roman Senate with the same ringing words: "Carthage must be destroyed! Carthage must be destroyed!" Finally, that great threat to Rome was vanquished, and Carthage was, indeed, destroyed. We must see ourselves in a great spiritual conflict, a conflict so serious that we can never think of negotiating a compromise. It is a conflict so serious that peaceful co-existence is impossible. Sin must be destroyed. Christ must conquer. We are His warriors."Onward, Christian soldiers!"

When Socrates was sentenced to death in Athens, his friends gathered. They offered him escape, but he refused to violate the laws of his beloved city. Quite calmly and with no sign of distaste, he took the poison and *drained* the cup! As he faced death with courage, we must face life with courage. As he saw principles worth dying for, we must see principles worth living for.

Remember that young David found that the armor of King Saul did not fit him. So he went to face Goliath without any armor at all. In a very different setting, we must ask if the armor of God fits us. If it does not, who is to blame? If it does not, what shall we do? The answer is that we must "grow into it." Did your parents always buy your clothing a little big so that it would last longer and then allow you to "grow into it"? Perhaps that is what God has done. He has made the armor a little large so that we may have room to grow!

Someone tasted the dark broth they served in the barracks of the Greek army and said, "Now I know why the Spartans do not fear death." Everyone knows why Christians do not fear death. They know theirs is a winning cause. They have complete and absolute confidence in the power and the promises of God.

"I am a man," said Terence, "and nothing human is alien to me." Even so, nothing human is beyond the concern of Christ. Therefore, nothing human is beyond the concern of Christians. We are concerned about the body, about hunger and starvation. We are concerned about the mind, about ignorance and falsehood. We are concerned about the emotions, about love and hate, fear and doubt. We are concerned about the spirit. We are convinced that the whole man must be treated; and sometimes the spirit must be treated before the body, the mind, or the heart. That is not always so, but it is sometimes so. We are open to all kinds of human need and ready to respond in the name and spirit of Christ.

SERMONS FROM COLOSSIANS

THE GOSPEL WE BELIEVE

Colossians 1:6, 25, 26; 3:16

Introduction:
A. How often we use this word, *gospel*
B. Do we really understand it and its effect upon the world?

Proposition: The church needs more fully to appreciate the wonder of the gospel.

I. THE SECRET WORD THAT GOD REVEALS, 1:25, 26
   A. It is from God.
   B. It has been unfolding throughout history.
   C. It is good news for *all* men.

II. THE SHARED WORD THAT MAN PROCLAIMS, 1:6
   A. It has the power of God.
   B. It has the power of truth.
   C. It has the power to bear fruit.

III. THE SUSTAINING WORD THAT WE RECEIVE, 3:16
   A. The gospel must dwell in the Christian.
   B. The gospel must be put into action.

Conclusion: When we see the wonder of the gospel, we have no trouble saying, "Speak, Lord, thy servant heareth."

During the early days of World War II, when the Nazis invaded France, the French citizens took down all the signposts. As the Nazi armies advanced, they did not know which way to turn or in what direction lay their objective. The signposts were taken down to confuse the enemy. Does it seem to you that the signposts of life have been taken down? They were not taken down by us to confuse the enemy, but were taken down by the enemy to confuse us. We do not know which way to turn until we turn to Scripture. The only reliable signposts are there.

God gradually reveals His truth, like a flower unfolding. It is not like the night-blooming cereus that opens only in the darkness and is seen by few. It is not like the century plant that opens so rarely and is seen so seldom. It is not like the morning glory that opens at dawn and is shut by noonday. God's revelation gradually unfolded; but it is now open for all to see. You may read the Bible night or day. At any time, in any place, you may look upon the beauty of God's opening of His heart to man.

"The pen is mightier than the sword." It's a familiar quotation. History has proven that it is true. Communism rules half the world today. Communism was advanced by the pen. Two documents, *Communist Manifesto* and *Das Kapital,* changed the world. It was the writing of Marx, Engles, and Lenin that put Communism on the map. If the written word of man is that powerful, how much more powerful must be the written Word of God!

Notre Dame Cathedral in Paris is one of the world's loveliest churches. There are four stained-glass windows. The east window is over the altar and depicts Jerusalem. The north window gets very little sun; so it depicts the Old Testament, when there was only a little spiritual light from God. The south window gets the most light; so it depicts Jesus, the Light of the world. The west window faces the sunset; so it depicts the end of the world. Notice that as we move from Old Testament to New, we move from darkness to light. With each generation, God shed more light on our path till the New Testament was completed and we could truly "walk in the light."

In commercial orchards, the setting of the fruit is no longer left to nature. When the tree is in just the right stage of bloom, the orchard is sprayed. The spray sets the fruit, and there is a better harvest. We often wonder why our lives are barren and unfruitful. We need God's Word in our lives to enable us to bear fruit. Only the gospel can do it.

He was an adult trying to learn Spanish. Whenever he saw a new book on the subject, he bought it. Wherever he found records on learning the language, he bought them. He owned every book in print on the subject of learning Spanish. He seemed to think that if he bought enough books, he would learn the language.

A minister visited once in the home of a spasmodic church attender. He found scores of books on religion. She brought them out by the armful. Apparently, she thought that if she owned books about Christ, she would be a Christian. Certainly, no one disputes the value of Christian books. Still, it is not the books we own that help us, but the books we read.

THE SAVIOR WE WORSHIP

Colossians 1:13-23

Introduction:
A. This world desperately needs to know Jesus.
B. To know Him, we must see Him as both human and divine.
C. We want to look at the divine side of Jesus; to see Him in His divine roles.

Proposition: Truly to understand Jesus, we must recognize His divine roles.

  I. CHRIST IS OUR REDEEMER, v. 14
    A. He has brought us into His kingdom.
    B. He has brought us out of the dominion of darkness.
    C. He has granted us forgiveness.

  II. CHRIST IS OUR CREATOR, vs. 15-17
    A. He is the image of God.
    B. All things were made by Him.
    C. All things were made for Him.
    D. All authority is His.

  III. CHRIST IS OUR RECONCILER, vs. 19-22
    A. God and man were separated.
    B. Sin was the cause.
    C. The cross was the cure.
    D. Peace is the prospect.

Conclusion: What a Savior we worship! What a life He offers!

Because Nazareth means *lily,* the new Church of the Annunciation in Nazareth has a steeple that resembles a lily. But it is an upside down lily, its open mouth pointing downward to suggest God's pouring out of himself to man. That is just what happened when Christ came. God's richest blessings were poured out upon us all.

Recently, a man in Danbury, Connecticut, defended himself in a murder case on the grounds that he was possessed by demons. That kind of defense was ruled inadmissable! It is true that evil has great power and influence, but it is also true that we have freedom of choice. We decide to come under the influence of evil or under the influence of Christ. We live in a dark world—dark with temptation, danger, anxiety, and fear. But we have the privilege of walking in the light.

When General Franco was the dictator of Spain, he often went to the palace to read his proclamations from the throne room. But he always stood beside the throne. He never sat on the throne of Spain. Christ, however, does not hesitate to occupy the throne at God's right hand nor to occupy His place as Head of His spiritual kingdom, the church.

Have you ever seen a child who was learning to walk reach up and take the hand of a parent? Have you seen him then, wanting more stability, reach up and take the hand of the other parent? It almost looks as if the child is drawing the parents together, as many a child has, indeed, done. Have you ever seen a friend trying to reconcile two enemies? He puts his hand on one arm of each and seems almost imperceptibly to draw them closer together. Have you ever seen the father of the bride take the hand of his daughter and the hand of the groom and draw them together? That is what Christ has done. He did it for Jew and Gentile. He did it for slave and master. He did it for male and female. He did it for man and God!

Constantine thought he had the original crown of thorns. He gave it to the Venetians as collateral for a loan! It was later bought by Louis IX of France. He built Paris' lovely cathedral of Saint Chapelle to house it and other relics he had purchased. Think of it! The crown of thorns as collateral for a loan! But wait a minute. The cross was more than collateral for our debt of sin. It paid the debt in full!

In *Star Wars*, Obi-Wan Kenobi meets Darth Vader. He says, "Now you must kill me, but know that in my death, I will defeat you." That is what Christ says to evil. "In my death, I will defeat you!" That is what He said to the vested interests that put Him to death: "In my death, I will defeat you!"

The Russian Orthodox church will not allow statues; but holy pictures, or icons, are acceptable. The most famous is the Virgin of Vladimir. Both Ivan the Terrible and Nicholas II carried it into battle. They believed they could not be defeated if the picture were taken to the battlefield. It is something quite different that we have in mind when we sing:

Onward, Christian soldiers,
Marching as to war;
With the cross of Jesus
Going on before.

THE CHURCH WE SERVE

Colossians 1:24-29

Introduction:
A. What does the church really need to come alive today?
B. Is it more programs?

Proposition: The church's need today is for dedicated persons.

I. BE A SERVANT OF THE WORD, vs. 24, 25
   A. The church needs more people with the humility of a servant.
   B. The church needs more people with the loyalty of a servant.
   C. The church needs more people with the industry of a servant.

II. BE A PROCLAIMER OF THE WORD, vs. 26-28
   A. Preach it.
   B. Teach it.
   C. Discuss it.

III. BE A CHANNEL FOR THE POWER, v. 29
   A. God is energizing the church.
   B. He needs people who will be channels for that energy.

Conclusion: The church needs people like this, people who will serve, proclaim, and energize the church.

He was staying in the elegant St. Francis Hotel in San Francisco. He went out in the street and stood looking into the window of a fancy jewelry store nearby. A shabbily dressed young couple came up and asked for money. "I'm sorry, I don't have any more either," he said. "Then come with us," was their reply, "and we'll give you part of what we get. We have some food and you can have half of that!" Often, it is not our substance we fail to share, but our Savior! It is not our money, but our Master that we selfishly keep to ourselves. It is not the staff of life that we hoard, but the bread of life! Let us say to a spiritually hungry world, "Come with us and share what we have!"

One of the earliest kings of England was called Ethelred the Unready! What an interesting name. Are there not some of his relatives still around? Don't some of his descendants belong to our churches? We are unready to serve, unready to share, unready to work, unready to study, and unready to pray!

Last Christmas, in Washington, D.C., someone rented a hall, hired an orchestra, and advertised a "sing-along" production of *The Messiah*. People stood in line to get tickets!

Five thousand did. They paid for the privilege of joining a giant choir to sing *The Messiah.* It is, in fact, a privilege to sing or speak for the Messiah. A minister once said that he was paid for a job which, if necessary, he would pay others for the privilege of doing! To tell someone of Christ is our greatest privilege. Why do we not take advantage of it? Suppose Christ had said to us, as He did to one long ago, "Tell no one I am the Messiah!" Wouldn't it be hard to keep such good news? How do we manage it?

Christchurch, New Zealand, boasts a very fine museum. Over the doorway are these words: "Lo, these are parts of His ways, but how little is heard of Him." Indeed! How little is heard of Him! The early Christians could not keep silent! Christians today cannot speak up! The threat of death could not silence those first believers. How are we so easily silenced? In our world, it is painfully true that "little is heard of Him." Let's change that!

We read so often of people who won't get involved in the problems of others. Here is a story that is different. In Palm Harbor, Florida, a van struck a car, and the car overturned. The van went on. But bystanders rushed to the car. They turned it right side up by hand. Out of nowhere, a doctor appeared and gave first aid to the occupant. Another motorist chased the van and later told the police where to find it. It was a grand demonstration of people caring about others, even when it was someone they did not know. That is the kind of caring that Christ would like to see in us all. Our caring must go beyond physical problems to spiritual needs, go beyond the body to the soul.

In some denominations, the minister follows a calendar that is called the church year. The year is divided into Advent and Pentecost and other seasons. There is a period called "ordinary time." Does it not seem to you that we are living in extraordinary times? Perhaps it has always seemed that way. Perhaps in every era people thought of their times as extraordinary times. Whether these are ordinary times or extraordinary times, the Word of God is appropriate. It will bless and strengthen.

THE MATURITY WE SEEK

Colossians 2:2-7

Introduction:
A. When we think of a mature church, what do we think of?
B. Paul was concerned about the Colossian church, that they would be a mature church.

Proposition: Paul says that there are certain marks of a mature church.

I. STAND TOGETHER IN LOVE, v. 2
   A. The church cannot proceed to other essential matters until it stands united.
   B. That unity can only be found in *love*.

II. STAND TALL IN WISDOM, vs. 3-5
   A. Of the mystery of God
   B. Of Christ
   C. Of His treasures of wisdom and knowledge

III. STAND FIRMLY IN FAITH, vs. 6, 7
   A. Receiving Christ is only the beginning; He continues His work in you.
   B. You must be rooted and built up in Him.
   C. You must be strengthened in faith.
   D. You must be overflowing in gratitude.

Conclusion: These signs of the mature church can only be found in Christ. Let Him lead you to be what you ought to be.

The emblem of the state of Kentucky shows two men facing each other, shaking hands. The motto beneath reads: "United we stand, divided we fall." That could also be the motto of any congregation. Could it perhaps be also a fitting motto for the church at large?

When a new minister was introduced for the first Sunday of his ministry, he was surprised and pleased to be greeted with sustained applause. Thanking them, he said that he hoped for a long ministry with them. He said that when there is applause at the beginning of a ministry, that's faith. When there is applause in the middle, that's hope. When there is applause at the end of a ministry, that's charity!

No church building in the world is more startling than the unfinished Sagrada Familial church in Barcelona, Spain. Already years into the building of it, it still will not be finished in this century. Great, frosted towers mount crazily toward the sky. There is no symmetry anywhere in this truly original design. The exterior resembles a randomly frosted cake. Four of the twelve towers are completed, but there is not a roof yet; and the vast structure is open to the skies. It is worth going a long way to see this most remarkable house

71

of worship ever built, and the most *avante garde.* But the doorway is finished; and over it is one Latin word, *"veritas."* Truth! That word could well be over the doorway of all our churches. Truth!

Whenever Ethiopian Emperor Menelik II was ill, he would eat a few pages from the Bible. He believed it would restore his health. He died in 1913, after eating the entire book of Kings.

The elder presiding at the little New Zealand church worked on the Cook Strait Ferry. Cook Strait lies between New Zealand's north and south islands. It is regarded as the second roughest ferry crossing in the world. Several times each week he crossed that wild sea. It was not surprising, then, that he announced as his favorite hymn the Sailor's Hymn:

> Eternal Father, strong to save,
> O hear us when we cry to Thee
> For those in peril on the sea.

THE ERRORS WE AVOID

Colossians 2:8-31

Introduction:
A. The Christian life has both positive and negative aspects.
B. Although positive, Christianity has to have negative restrictions at times.

Proposition: In our Christian lives, there are many pitfalls to avoid.

I. THE SHALLOWNESS OF HUMAN PHILOSOPHY, vs. 8-11
   A. It is empty.
   B. It is based on tradition.
   C. It leaves out Christ.

II. THE SHADOWS OF LEGALISM, vs. 11-19
   A. Salvation of the cross is superior.
   B. Legalism tears the believer down.
   C. The Old Law was but a shadow.

III. THE SUBSTANCE OF THE GOSPEL, vs. 19-21
   A. It frees us from human regulations.
   B. It fastens us to Christ our head.
   C. It enables us to grow.

Conclusion: If we avoid the pitfalls and remain close to Christ, we can be complete in Him.

Many think that baseball's famous threesome, "Tinker to Evers to Chance," was the greatest double-play combination in the history of baseball. They were good; but they have been somewhat over-rated. There have been many infielders far, far better. It was a poem that brought them more fame than they deserved. The poem was written by Franklin P. Adams in 1910 for a New York newspaper; and that led to the legend of "Tinker to Evers to Chance." The power of the press is enormous; but the power of truth is stronger. Many false ideas are in the world about man, life, religion, and the soul. Some of them are widely held for a time. But truth eventually must conquer error.

A man put this sign in front of his auto repair shop: "Beware of bargains in life rafts, brain surgery, parachutes, and auto repairs." There are truly some points in life at which bargains are no good. When cultists came calling on a man in one village, he said, "Come in. You're offering me a better deal than I'm getting up there at the church!" We must go beyond that which looks good to find real value, to find the truth, to find God's truth!

A recent cartoon showed a teenage boy talking to a teenage girl. He was saying, "I may be a little weak on opinions and convictions, but my prejudices are as strong as anybody's."

In Harry Reasoner's book, *Before the Colors Fade,* Reasoner wrote an article about Christmas. He called it "The Truest Thing in the World." That can be said of the whole gospel. It is the truest thing in the world. Many ideas may hold some truth. They may be partially true or even temporarily true. The gospel, however, is "the truth, the whole truth, and nothing but the truth." It is indeed, "the truest thing in the world."

A little sandpiper, flying high above the Mississippi River, can hear the surf from both the Atlantic and the Pacific coasts! Do we try to tune our ears in two directions? Do we try to keep one ear attuned for the voice of God and the other for the call of the world? It won't do! We must tune out the earthly frequencies and let God alone direct our path.

Hans Christian Andersen wrote of a mirror that made every good and pretty thing look bad. Do not many of us have just such a distorted view of life? Good looks bad; and bad looks good. We must come instead to the true mirror of God's Word and see things as He sees them. Then we shall see them as they truly are.

In many northern cities, when spring melts the snow and cars splash the slush, road crews must come along and scrub the street signs. They've become obscured! For many, the spiritual street signs have been covered by human ideas and opinions and prejudices. We need to wash all that off and see what directions God has given us.

THE NEW LIFE WE CAN ENJOY

Colossians 3:2-17

Introduction: To use something new, the old must go. If we want new life, the old must go.

Proposition: The Christian life involves a putting off and a putting on.

I. THE OLD WAYS THAT MUST BE ELIMINATED, vs. 5-9.
   A. Improper sexual desires
   B. Improper worship
   C. Improper temperament
   D. Improper communication

II. THE NEW WAYS THAT MUST BE CULTIVATED, vs. 12-14
   A. Mercy
   B. Kindness
   C. Meekness
   D. Patience
   E. Forgiveness
   F. And, above all, love

Conclusion: Salvation is not just for canceling out the past; it is also for enhancing the present and the future. We must put off and put on certain things. Our whole life must be lived in the name of Christ.

It is interesting that one of the sub-culture groups in our day has adopted the bunny as its symbol. This is the completely sex-oriented group that took its cue from Hugh Heffner and his Playboy Clubs. Now a rabbit can only do three things: eat, reproduce, and run away! Have you ever played the parlor game that asks what animal you would like to be? Some would like to be an owl, very wise. Some would like to be a turtle, long lived. Some would like to be a bird and soar and sing. But who would want to be a rabbit? A dumb, cowardly rabbit!

There are places in the United States where it is considered a mild insult to call a man "boy." It was once a goal of every person to be thought a man or a woman. Against this context, we must read the titles of today's pornography magazines, *PlayBOY* and *PlayGIRL*. They are well named. Their readers are immature, childish, and pathetic!

In Paris, *Montemarte* means mount of the martyrs. At its foot, the streets are lined with porno shops!

It is a common expression among golfers, as one approaches the ball he has just hit onto the green, "How do you lie?" Sometimes one questions the answer and changes the question to an exclamation, "How you do lie!" In fact, there are some cynical souls who trust no one. Many do lie; but there are also many who will always tell you the truth.

Have you ever seen one of those startling sentences lettered on a truck or van, "Blind Man Driving!" Then you realize that it is a man who sells venetian blinds! Or, the equally atrocious pun you see in some dry cleaner ads: "We dye to live." All of us must die to live; not d-y-e, but d-i-e. Over and over again in his letters, Paul uses death as the best illustration of the radical change that comes into our lives when we accept Christ. The changes are so great that only terms like death and resurrection can describe them.

Stephen Judy was convicted of murdering a twenty-three-year-old mother and her three children. Interviewed two days before his execution, he said, "I can't say I regret it, honestly. I don't lose any sleep over it."

Again and again, God demonstrates that He can bring good out of evil. The Black Plague was a great evil; but had there been no Black Plague, there would have been no Passion Play at Oberammergau. This village, threatened by the Plague more than three hundred years ago, prayed to be spared. They vowed that if they were, they would put on a play to honor Christ and would do it every ten years till the end of time. The vow has been kept, and thousands upon thousands have been inspired by the Passion Play.

THE PRAYERS WE OFFER

Colossians 4:2

Introduction:
A. Many complain of a weak prayer life.
B. It is a universal need we have to pray more effectively.

Proposition: Christians need a more vital prayer life.

I. DISCIPLINED PRAYERS
   A. Pray often.
   B. Pray regularly.
   C. Pray spontaneously.

II. WATCHFUL PRAYERS (literally wakeful)
    A. Aware of our purpose.
    B. Aware of His purpose.

III. THANKFUL PRAYERS
     A. Thankful for His past blessings
     B. Thankful for His present blessings.
     C. Thankful for His future blessings.

Conclusion: With these three characteristics, our prayer lives will come alive.

Dial-A-Prayer has been around for years. Recently, the Tampa Bay (Florida) chapter of American Atheists installed a 24-hour telephone called "Dial-An-Atheist." We wonder if anyone burdened by guilt, anxiety, or fear will seek comfort from "Dial-An-Atheist." Most churches in the area are not worried about the competition!

He said that he was the guest speaker at a Kiwanis Club. In front of the podium was a little bank of flags that included a tiny American flag. When it came time to pledge allegiance to the flag, the lectern completely obscured the flag from those at the head table. Everyone else could see it; but those at the head table had to pledge in faith, believing that a flag was really there. We pray in faith. We cannot see God. We cannot feel the muscle of His mighty arm. We pray in faith; but God rewards our faith and responds to our prayer.

It does not always pay to pray. In Caribou County, British Columbia, a man was accused of setting a forest fire. Left alone in a room of the police department, he fell to his knees and prayed, "Oh God, please let me get away with it!" The prayer was picked up by a closed circuit television camera and microphone. The trial judge would not let the prosecutor introduce that as evidence. But when the case was appealed, it was admitted into evidence and used against him.

Sometimes people change the locks on their apartment doors or their office doors. Then the old key won't work anymore. Nobody has changed the locks in Heaven. Prayer is still the key that opens Heaven's door. It always has been and it always will be. Whether you have a fond memory of that little chorus from childhood or not, you still need to know:

> Prayer is the key
> That opens Heaven's door.

Of all the Jewish sects, the most interesting is the Hasidic. Their adherents are found chiefly in Brooklyn and Jerusalem. They are, in some ways, the most conservative of Jews, but there are surprises. They have made dance an important part of their worship. In fact, the founder of Hasidm said, "A dance is better than a prayer if it comes from the heart." Probably few Jews would agree with that. But we all agree that the prayer that does not come from the heart is worthless—and the prayer that does come from the heart is of inestimable value.

The Minister of Music had changed the order of service, and he wanted to be sure there would be no mistake. So he whispered to the preacher, "After the prayer, there will be no response." Doesn't it sometimes seem to you that after the prayer, there is no response? It may seem that way; but it is not that way. It is not if we pray in faith. It is not if we pray in the name of Jesus. There is always a response! It may not be the response we wanted. It may not be the response we hoped for. But after the prayer, there is always a response!

THE PARTNERSHIP WE SHARE

Colossians 4:5-18

Introduction: Sometimes people have themselves incorporated for legal or tax purposes. The Christian relationship is not at all like a corporation; but it is a great deal like a partnership.

Proposition: We are never alone in serving Christ; we have partners who are both like us and unlike us.

I. THE EARLY CHRISTIANS HAD DIFFERING BACK-GROUNDS
   A. There were Greeks and Jews.
   B. There were free persons and slaves.
   C. There were males and females.
   D. The church today is enriched by the great variety of nationalities, races, and cultures that are part of it.

II. THEY HAD DIFFERING GIFTS
   A. There are public gifts and private gifts.
   B. They are of equal importance and significance.
   C. All are needed.

III. THEY HAD DIFFERING DUTIES
   A. Communication
   B. Encouragement
   C. Comfort
   D. Prayer

IV. THEY HAD THE SAME PURPOSE AND GOAL
   A. All were family in Christ.
   B. All were servants of Christ.

Conclusion: We need each other. We need Christ most of all.

During the times of the New Testament, there was great enmity between Jews and Romans. They had as little dealings with one another as possible and, whenever they could, avoided using the same streets! We cannot imagine such prejudice! The good news is that Christ overcame that prejudice and pride—and He still does.

It has been well said that the man who holds the ladder at the bottom is about as important as the man at the top. Everybody wants to be the man on the top, but he would not be there very long without the assistance he receives from the man at the bottom. If he is wise, the man at the top will recognize the importance of the man at the bottom. If he does not recognize it, he may find his ladder slipping away!

When Anwar Sadat, of Egypt, was assassinated, they provided a temporary burial place beside Egypt's Unknown Soldier. How interesting that Egypt's best-known soldier should be buried beside Egypt's Unknown Soldier! In the kingdom of God, there are many unknown soldiers. They march right beside the well-known soldiers. They do their parts. What they do is important! Without their work, the famous would not be famous! Without them, nothing would be accomplished!

Lyman Bryson wrote: "The error of youth is to believe that intelligence is a substitute for experience, while the error of age is to believe that experience is a substitute for intelligence." Doesn't that point up the fact that we need both young and old in our churches? We need the optimism and enthusiasm of youth. We need the experience and wisdom of age. One tempers the other. It is so easy to go off optimistically without thinking through the ramifications of a problem. It is equally easy to be content with things as they are and not see the possibilities for improvement.

Carl Sandburg was one of our greatest poets. He flunked English. Thomas Edison was our greatest inventor. His teachers thought he was stupid. Einstein was our greatest intellect. He could not speak until he was four and did not read until he was seven. Beethoven is the world's best-known composer. His music teacher said, "As a composer, he's hopeless." F. W. Woolworth has his name on stores all over the nation. When he was twenty-one, he couldn't get a job. The boss thought he didn't have enough sense to wait on customers. Walt Disney was fired by a newspaper editor because he didn't have any good ideas. Caruso was told by his voice coach, "You can't sing. You have no voice at all." An editor told Louisa May Alcott she was not capable of writing anything that would appeal to the popular audience. Obviously, all these critics were wrong in their judgments of the possibilities in the lives of others. How quickly we prejudge and misjudge! How often we are wrong! How often we value our own gifts so much we cannot see how very valuable are the gifts of others!

God give my eyes the will to see
My friend for what he is to me.
It's not his creed or shade or skin
That makes his heart to mine akin;
O God, if peace on earth we seek,
Our hearts must follow Yours so meek;
And see ourselves as no other,
But to every man—a brother.

Vivian Volk

SERMONS FROM PHILIPPIANS

LIVE WITH JOY

Philippians 1:1-11

Introduction:
A. Paul, in the midst of his imprisonment, wrote a book of joy.
B. How could Paul be joyful in such bleak circumstances?

Proposition: To find joy, we must look for it in the simple things around us.

I. FIND JOY IN PEOPLE, vs. 3, 4, 7-9
   A. Their diversities
   B. Their possibilities

II. FIND JOY IN PRAYER, vs. 4, 9
   A. Unselfish prayer
   B. Specific prayer

III. FIND JOY IN PARTNERSHIP, vs. 5-7
   A. Not bound by distance
   B. Not bound by time
   C. Not bound by differences

IV. FIND JOY IN PRODUCTIVITY, v. 9
   A. Abound in love
   B. Abound in knowledge and wisdom
   C. Abound in purity

Conclusion: We have been talking about finding joy. There is, however, a sense in which we let joy find us.

Towering over Edinburgh, Scotland, is the Edinburgh Castle. In the midst of very old buildings is the relatively new World War I Memorial. It carries a quotation from Thucydides: "The whole earth is the tomb of heroic men, and their story is not graven only on stones over their clay, but abides everywhere, without visible symbol, woven into the stuff of others' lives."

In his book, *Daily Thoughts for Disciples,* Oswald Chambers writes, "We take for granted that prayer is preparation for work, whereas prayer is *the* work. Intercessory prayer is God's chosen way of working."

You can carry a pack if it's strapped to your back;
You can carry a weight in your hands.
You can carry a bundle on top of your head
   As they do in other lands.
A load is light if you carry it right,
Though it weighs as much as a boulder;
But a tiny chip is too heavy to bear
   If you carry it on your shoulder.

A few years ago, no television personality was better known than Gary Moore. He once gave his own philosophy of life. He said that if on every day you could count one half hour of real happiness, then you were ahead of the game! Where can we find happiness? Or is it a matter of letting happiness finding us?

The old physician kept up his practice well into his 80's. He walked a lot, and as he walked, he picked up string, bolts, and nails. All of these he carefully stashed away in manila envelopes. When he died, they found them among his possessions. Each envelope was marked the same: "MCH." They wondered what that meant until it was finally discovered the "MCH" stood for "may come in handy." We need to cultivate friendships: they may come in handy. We need to nourish spiritual partnerships: they may come in handy.

Though he served during very difficult years, Franklin Roosevelt never seemed to worry. The ebullience he displayed on stage was really a part of his personality all the time. Once he was asked if he ever worried. He replied by referring to the polio that had left him a cripple: "If you had spent two years in bed trying to wiggle your toe, after that anything would seem easy."

Recently, Parker and Hart's comic strip, "The Wizard of Id," showed a lonely and bored little king who finally sighed from his balcony, "It's lonely at the top." And a voice from below answered, "It ain't no bed of roses at the bottom, Charlie!"

It has well been said that "the road to a friend's house is never long."

Square Deal Surf is a detergent made in Britain. The company decided to stop advertising and pass the savings along to the customer. They reduced the price of the product and increased the weight of the package. Sales dropped. They resumed advertising, increasing the price and reducing the amount in the box. Sales increased! It pays to advertise.

After a great gathering of Christian youth, they were counting the offering. At the bottom lay a teen-aged girl's picture. Had someone taken that picture from someone's wallet and thrown it in the offering as a practical joke? That's the kind of thing teenagers sometimes do. But someone turned the picture over. On the back of her own picture, a girl had written, "I have nothing to give but myself." Whether we have little to give or much to give, the gift God wants us to give is ourselves!

LIVE WITH PERSPECTIVE

Philippians 1:12-30

Introduction:
A. One of the hardest lessons to learn in life is what is important and what isn't.
B. One of the reasons Paul was able to withstand so much was that he knew where to place his priorities.
 I. HIS MISSION MATTERED MORE THAN HIS PROBLEMS, vs. 12-14
   A. Problems
     1. Health problems
     2. Family problems
     3. Economic problems
     4. Social problems
   B. Victory
     1. His problems served to advance the gospel.
     2. His problems served to inspire others.
 II. HIS MESSAGE MATTERED MORE THAN HIS PRIDE, vs. 15-18
   A. Pride
     1. National pride
     2. Religious pride
     3. Community pride
     4. Personal pride
   B. Victory
     1. The gospel can be preached from dual motives.
     2. It can be preached amid misunderstandings.
III. HIS MASTER MATTERED MORE THAN HIS PERSON, vs. 19-26
   A. His Person
     1. Threatened
     2. Tortured
     3. Endangered
   B. Victory
     1. His master gave him meaning for life.
     2. His master gave him meaning in death.
Conclusion: In death or life, all that mattered to Paul was that his master be glorified.

Queen Mary of England was so upset by the French capture of the Port of Calais that she could never get it off her mind. She said, "After I am dead, you will find Calais written upon my heart." Well could one say of Paul that Christ was written on his heart. What is written on your heart? What is most important in your life?

Often in life, we give up a present benefit for a larger future benefit. The student gives up his leisure for the sake of an education. The lover gives up his freedom for the security of marriage. The dieter gives up foods he likes for the sake of health and a longer life. The person in the military gives up civilian life for the benefit of his military career. The jogger gives up comfort for health. The saver gives up some purchases for the sake of a larger one later on. That is what separates man from animals. Cattle will eat until they die. Paul saw the larger eternal benefits and gave up the present, smaller benefits.

The glory had gone to Napoleon, but he could never have accomplished what he did without Marshal Ney, his most brilliant and his most courageous officer. They called Marshal Ney "the bravest of the brave." Certainly, Paul deserves such a description.

It was the tranquil scene on the calendar that first caught the eye. Then the verse, "Today is the tomorrow we worried about yesterday." We do spend a lot of time worrying about tomorrow. Most of our worries are useless. We may spend so much time worrying about tomorrow that we miss the opportunities of the present. Many of us live by an inversion of the old motto. Ours is "Never do today what can be put off till tomorrow."

A minister recently wrote in his weekly column in the church newsletter that he was setting goals for the new year. One of his goals was to clean up his desk. Another of his goals was to find last year's goals!

His name is Wersching, and he is the great place kicker of the San Francisco Forty-Niners. He never looks at the goal posts. They distract him. He only looks at the hash marks on the field. With Paul, it was much the opposite. He kept his eye on the goal. Anything between him and that didn't matter much.

100

In writing an article on death, a minister noted that he had just taken a course in thanatology, the study of death. Well, life itself is a course in death. Joseph Addision, near death, sent for his stepson. When he arrived, Addison said, "I have sent for you that you may see how a Christian can die." In Gloucester, England, is a tombstone with this oddly splendid epitaph:

> Death Comes Apace
> The Indignant Nye
> Go Reader Go
> And Learn to Dye

We all must learn how to die—*and* how to live!

The most conservative of Jewish sects and the most interesting is the Hasidic. Found principally in Brooklyn and Jerusalem, they are fiercely opposed to Zionism and fanatically devoted to Jewish ritual and custom. Yet dance is a part of their worship—joyous dance; for the founder of Hasidism said, "To be sad is a sin."

LIVE WITH HUMILITY

"Living the Life of Christ"

Philippians 2:1-11

Introduction: Our age tells us to look out for number one. It glorifies those who have power and know how to use it. Yet Jesus said he who would be greatest should be servant of all. Paul must have learned humility from Christ.

Proposition: The Christian must understand the benefits of humility and the source of humility.

I. THE EFFECT OF HUMILITY, vs. 1-4
   A. You can achieve unity (not uniformity).
      1. You can find motivation for living.
      2. You can find comfort in His love.
      3. You can find fellowship in His Spirit.
      4. You can find goodness.
   B. You can control ambition.
   C. You can ease boasting.
   D. You can display honor.
   E. You can show concern.

II. THE EXAMPLE OF HUMILITY, vs. 5-11
   A. The status He surrendered
   B. The service He offered
   C. The sacrifice He endured
   D. The supremacy He commands

Conclusion: In humility we honor Christ.
             In humility we minister to each other.
             In humility we receive joy.

Among the interesting motto T-shirts created lately is this one that fits our times: "Woman has to do twice as much as a man to be considered half as good. Fortunately, it's not difficult."

The boxer who is now known as Muhammed Ali began life as Cassius Clay. When he reached fame, he changed his name. He said Clay was a name that came from slavery and he would not wear it any longer. What he did not know was this: *THE* Cassius Clay for whom he was named was a fiery opponent of slavery. He opposed it at a time when it was quite dangerous to do so. On the other hand, the original Muhammed Ali had done nothing to replace slavery with freedom! In his pride, the boxer had displayed his ignorance, spurned the man who helped his people's cause, and named himself after a man who had done nothing for it at all!

There is a time-honored custom in the Syrian Orthodox Church. A basin of water is brought, and the bishop washes the feet of the choir boys. Even symbolic humility may be instructive, but our minds run to a more practical humility. We need to be humble enough to wash feet that are dirty, not feet already clean; to do it practically, not just symbolically. To reach out to the world's hurting, hungry people and never think ourselves too important to serve them. Jesus, on the night before the world's most significant event, did not think himself too important to wash the disciples' feet!

Robert Goizueta is the president of the Coca-Cola Company. He likes to quote Henry Ford. Ford said, "You can't build a reputation on what you're going to do." Commenting on that quotation, Goizueta said, "We must lead by example first, then by precept." That is exactly what Jesus has done. He leads us by example.

Rivers gain more attention than the little streams that create them. You can name the great rivers of the world, but you cannot name their tributaries. However, without the tributaries, there would be no river. And it must be remembered that the smaller streams, while less well-known, are purer and are found on a higher elevation. Some of our lives are tributary lives. It is our role to provide the pure water from the higher elevation that enables another to be a mighty river of power and influence.

It was just shortly after the resurrection. Jesus must have had many very important things to do. Yet He took the time to gather some sticks, build a fire, and cook breakfast for the disciples beside the sea. It is amazing that He should do that. We think ourselves too important for the menial tasks of life. We say that we have such important things to do that these must be left for others. But Jesus, in a superb example of humility, came from the victory of the resurrection to the simple task of building a fire and cooking breakfast.

Sadly, we get our ideas of humility from Uriah Heep, in the novels of Dickens, or from Casper Milquetoast in the comics, and not from Jesus, and Moses, and Paul. Biblical humility must be understood in the light of Biblical lives, not in fiction or fantasy.

LIVE WITH PURPOSE

Philippians 2:12-21

Introduction: Many people want a minimal level Christianity. God is looking for people who will go beyond the minimum, who don't want just barely to make it to Heaven.

Proposition: There is a glorious challenge in the life to which Christ calls us.

  I. I AM WILLING TO DO MORE, vs. 12, 13
     A. Man's part—to submit
     B. God's part—to empower

  II. I AM WILLING TO SHINE MORE, vs. 14-16
     A. Shine in my moral convictions
     B. Shine in my willingness to share the Word

  III. I AM WILLING TO CARE MORE, vs. 19-29
     A. Genuine concern
     B. Christian concern

  IV. I AM WILLING TO RISK MORE, v. 17
     A. Why risk anything?
     B. How much will I risk?

Conclusion: God saw in us something that made it worthwhile to take a risk, even in the light of our sins. If Christ was willing to risk all for us, then we must risk all for Him.

We eat foods that do not nourish us. We drink beverages that do not quench our thirst. We wear clothing that does not protect us. They all symbolize the fact that we live without purpose. Life has no more meaning for many than it has for the squirrel in his cage, turning his little wheel. God wants to give high purpose to life. He wants to challenge us to give our lives to the same noble purposes to which Jesus gave His life.

All across our country, there are amateur weather observers who cooperate with the National Weather Service by providing data on daily weather conditions in their area. The oldest of these is Edward H. Stoll, a Nebraska farmer who has been recording daily weather conditions for seventy-four years. Recently, he was honored in Washington. Upon leaving the White House, Stoll said, "You owe service to somebody else, not just yourself. Service is the rent that you pay for the space that you occupy as you go through life."

In the Book of Numbers, you will read that the Gershonites and the Merarites were given wagons to transport their goods. But the Kohathites had no wagons, for they carried holy things. It was required that they carry them on their shoulders! God honors us when He gives us responsibilities in His church and in His world. Holy things must always be carried personally!

Veteran India missionaries Archie and Maggie Watters recalled that when a man in India became a Christian, he cut off his hair, his pig tail that had been a symbol of his old faith. It was a sign to the community that he had renounced the old pagan religion and had accepted Christ. We have more subtle ways to do that in our culture, but it must be done. Loving service must be the symbol of our new relationship.

Roberto C. Goizueta rose from the ranks to become the president of the Coca-Cola Company, one of the world's largest business enterprises. One of his favorite sayings is from the Japanese writer Mishima: "To know and not to act is not yet to know." He has made that a guiding principle of his life. His advice to young managers is, "Do the best you can, and a little bit more. The rest will take care of itself."

Queen Anne had seventeen children in the hope of having a successor to the throne of England. None of them survived her; and what she most feared happened. Her German cousin became king of England.

Bishop Moore of the Methodist Church used to say, "I'd rather try to restrain a fanatic than resurrect a corpse."

Michelangelo started forty-four statues, but completed only fourteen. In a museum in Italy, you can see his thirty unfinished works. There are huge chunks of marble with only a hand, or a foot, or a leg completed. Are our lives like those unfinished statues? Is the potential for beauty and purpose still locked up within us as those figures are locked in the stone?

LIVE WITH INSIGHT

"A New Vision"

Philippians 3:2-11

Introduction: Sight and insight are not the same. Insight looks beyond the immediate, looks beneath the surface, looks into the heart.

Proposition: Understanding Christ is essential to understanding the Christian religion and to understanding life itself.

I. INSIGHT INTO THE VALUE OF CHRIST, vs. 7, 8
    A. What was profit is now loss.
    B. What was treasure is now trash.
    C. What was great is now garbage.

II. INSIGHT INTO THE RIGHTEOUSNESS OF CHRIST, v. 9
    A. A righteousness which can be imparted
    B. A righteousness whose foundation is faith

III. INSIGHT INTO THE POWER OF CHRIST, v. 10
    A. Really to know Christ, you must understand His resurrection.
    B. That same power is at work today.

IV. INSIGHT INTO THE SUFFERING OF CHRIST, v. 10
    A. In suffering, Christ abides with us.
    B. In suffering, Christ teaches us.
    C. In suffering, Christ blesses us.

Conclusion: The power for conversion is resurrection power.

Did you ever know anyone with double vision? It is most disconcerting. Spiritually, though, we all need double vision. We must see God and man, Heaven and earth, the present and the future. We must look to God for our inspiration; and we must look about us for the work we need to do.

Someone wrote, "If you have a well-developed sense of humor, you will find the world full of absurdities. If you are a realist, you will find it a world of cold, hard facts. If you are a money maker, you will find it a world of opportunities. If you are a pessimist, you will find it just a climb up a sand dune. And if you are a poet, you will find it a realm of inspiration."

In Tarpon Springs, Florida, Greek Christians gather each year at Epiphany for a festival seen nowhere else in the United States. The archbishop of the Orthodox Church throws a gold cross into the waters of Spring Bayou. Young men dive for it. The one who finds it is supposed to receive good luck throughout the coming year. One year, reporters interviewed the boy who recovered the cross the previous year. "Did you have any good luck?" they asked. "Well—well," hesitated the boy, "I didn't have any bad luck!"

A reproduction of a very old and famous clock carries this line: "Lord, through this hour be thou our guide; so by thy power no foot shall slide." What insight Christ gives us into temptation. How He enables us to see the snares laid for our souls!

A famous photographer said he always took his camera when the family went on vacation. They teased him about looking at the world through a view finder. One year, he dropped his camera in the water the first day out. The family said it was their best vacation ever. He said, "For the first time, I saw the world in a larger view than that of a camera."

The most famous clock in the world is London's Big Ben. It stands by the House of Parliament and towers above Westminster Abbey. It is a familiar landmark to everyone. The chimes of Big Ben play the tune of a hymn. The hymn is "I Know That My Redeemer Liveth"!

Visitors to the Holy Land enjoy seeing the ancient cathedrals; but they are also impressed by some of the newer churches. One of these is the lovely Church of the Annunciation in Nazareth. There is hardly a picture of the city without it. The spire is a representation of a light house, for Jesus is the Light of the world!

All of the skyscrapers in New York City were built by Indians! Yes, Mohawk Indians are native to New York State. They are famed for their cat-like ability to scamper across girders. They are totally indifferent to heights. It seems to be a genetic trait. In 1714, a writer spoke of it. In 1886, they built the bridge that spans the St. Lawrence River. They were the riveters of the Empire State Building and the Rockefeller Center. Some people are uncomfortable in such high places, but the Mohawk Indians seem right at home. Spiritual heights are uncomfortable for some. They want to live in the lowlands of life. Christ keeps calling us to higher ground. As we learn to live in the rarefied air of spiritual heights in this life, we prepare ourselves for the climate of Heaven.

Lord, lift me up and let me stand
By faith on Heaven's tableland.
A higher plane than I have found
Lord, plant my feet on higher ground.

LIVE WITH DETERMINATION

"Pressing On"

Philippians 3:12-21

Introduction:
A. Life is a challenge.
B. It is so challenging that it requires a great deal of discipline and determination.

Proposition: It takes effort to maintain a right relationship with Christ.

  I. MOVING AHEAD, vs. 12-14
    A. Keep your mind on your goal.
    B. Keep your mind off the past.
    C. Keep your mind off the difficulties.
    D. Keep your mind off yourself.

  II. STAYING AHEAD, vs. 15-17
    A. Don't grow weary.
    B. Don't give up.
    C. Don't be complacent.

  III. LOOKING AHEAD, vs. 18-21
    A. There are only two choices.
    B. One choice is to live as an "enemy of Christ"
      1. Their desire
      2. Their destiny
    C. The better choice is to live as a "citizen of Heaven"
      1. Their hope
      2. Their help

Conclusion: The rewards are great for those who are willing to pay the price.

Augustus boasted of Rome that he found it a city of bricks and left it a city of marble. Perhaps we cannot look at the world and find that we leave it much different than we found it. But surely we can look at life and say that we had some influence, taken some opportunity, made some improvements.

In a single day, Guthrie, Oklahoma, became a city of 10,000. That was the time when Indian territories were first opened to settlement. Can you imagine a city growing so large so fast? Think of the problems. We sometimes expect too much too soon. When that fails, we become defeated, complacent, or indifferent, and we stop expecting any improvement. Somewhere there is a balance between expecting too much too soon and having no expectations at all.

A minister said he received an announcement of a new magazine that would make him more efficient in his work. They sent him four identical letters in the same mail! They wanted to help him be efficient but had overlooked a gross inefficiency of their own. We want to help others, and we want to develop ourselves.

Islanders on Andros Island in the Bahamas believe in a spirit called Chickcharnee. Some say they have seen him in the forested interiors of the island. They say that if you see him, you must not laugh. If you do, he will turn your head around backward. That has already happened to some people. All they can see is the past. They are either weeping over past failures or glorying over past achievements, but it is all in the past. They have their heads turned around backward.

On the Hawaiian island of Maui is a church with a most unusual story. A storm struck the island and deposited enough coral to build a stone church. When it was finished, another storm came up and washed the leftover coral back to sea. They call it the miracle church! We can expect no such convenient miracles to take the place of our own effort and service.

God sends no churches from the skies;
Out of men's hearts they must arise.

Along the Danube River, on top of a prominent hill, is the famous Weissenkirk, with 365 steps leading up to it from the valley below. So there may be many steps to reaching our spiritual goals, whether they are personal goals or collective goals for our congregation. We must not get discouraged. We must take one step at a time.

They once bragged that all roads led to Rome. It was not true, of course, It is never true that all roads lead to the same destination. In life, we must choose our roads carefully and inquire as to their destination. When we come to a crossroads, we must assume that those two roads certainly do not lead to the same place. We must look for the signposts and make our choices wisely.

LIVE WITH POWER

Philippians 4:1-13

Introduction: Ours is a power-conscious age. Every age has been a power-conscious age.

Proposition: We must see the various aspects of the spiritual power we have available.

  I. THE POWER OF COOPERATION, vs. 1-3
     A. The priority of it
     B. The urgency of it

  II. THE POWER OF COMMUNICATION, vs. 4-7
     A. The scope of prayer
     B. The attitude in prayer
     C. The blessing from prayer

  III. THE POWER OF CONCENTRATION, vs. 8, 9
     A. Focus on things true
     B. Focus on things honorable
     C. Focus on things just
     D. Focus on things pure
     E. Focus on things lovely
     F. Focus on things gracious

  IV. THE POWER OF CONTENTMENT, vs. 10-13
     A. Content in spite of circumstances
     B. Content because of Christ

Conclusion: God gives us these amazing powers. Let us receive these gifts with thanksgiving and use them daily.

It ain't no use to trouble and complain;
It's better far to be happy and rejoice!
When God sorts out the weather and sends rain—
Rain's my choice!

Every day begins in beauty! We begin our days with sleep-filled eyes and empty stomachs. Our blood pressure is low and our blood sugar is low and our disposition is even lower. But God enables us to begin every day with beauty; for every day begins with sunrise and bird song. With visual beauty and with audible beauty, every day dawns. If only we had eyes to see and ears to hear!

Someone once wrote: "The will of God will never lead you where the grace of God cannot keep you." That's another way of saying, with Paul, that we never have temptations greater than we can bear. We so often pray for lighter burdens when we ought to pray for stronger shoulders. We pray for an easier path when we ought to pray for tougher feet. We pray for fewer problems when we ought to pray for better solutions. We pray for easier tasks when we ought to pray for stronger muscles. We pray for calm when we ought to face the storm and ride it out.

When a storm comes at sea, a ship turns to face the tempest. If the vessel allows the storm to hit its side, it will capsize. If it turns its back to the storm, the storm will drive it wherever the wind blows. But the ship faces the storm and is safe. The storms of life must be faced. We dare not leave them to one side, nor turn and run from them. Facing them is our only safety.

Sometimes life boxes us in. We cannot always choose our circumstances. But we can always choose the way we react to our circumstances. We cannot always change things outwardly, but we have ever the power to change things inwardly.

Rabbi Harold Kushner found it difficult to accept his son's illness. He was told that his bright three-year-old had a rare disease that caused premature aging. He would not live beyond his teens. As the Rabbi watched his son grow bald, and wrinkled, and arthritic over eleven years, he wrestled with the basic questions of life. He searched the Bible, and he searched his own soul. The result was a book, *When Bad Things Happen to Good People*. In it, he shows that the painful things of life are not a punishment, nor are they

God's will for us personally. They are rather the result of the kind of world we live in. If we could, we would choose to avoid them; but we grow by them. Thus, in working through his own pain, he was able to help others who suffer.

If an army marches on its stomach, a church marches on its knees! We must never lose our line of communication with God. The hour we devote to prayer has been called the most powerful hour of the day. World Vision holds sessions across the country called a "School of Prayer." Jesus led a school of prayer when His disciples came saying, "Teach us to pray." Jesus and Paul and the early Christians teach us by their example that we must not break our lines of communication with God.

A SERMON FROM PHILEMON

CHANGES IN THE LINEUP

Philemon 1-15

Introduction: No book in the Bible is more surprising than Philemon, and none is more practical.

Proposition: A new relationship with Christ changes our human relationships.

I. PAUL HAS A NEW SON
   A. Begotten by the gospel
   B. Born from above
   C. Brought into the Christian family

II. PHILEMON HAS A NEW BROTHER
   A. They share the same mentor—Paul.
   B. They share the same task—Evangelism.
   C. They share the same bond—Love.
   D. They share the same faith in God.

III. ONESIMUS HAS A NEW MASTER
   A. God takes priority over the old master.
   B. He does not eliminate the old relationship.
   C. He puts new light on the old relationship.
   D. He adds a new dimension to the old relationship.

Conclusion: Human relationships are important, but the most important relationship is that between you and God.

If you visit Nashville, Tennessee, you will likely also visit the Hermitage, the home of Andrew Jackson. Andrew Jackson, the man who transformed American politics, put his own indelible stamp on government. He is remembered as "Old Hickory," a rough and tough, hard-fighting man. A different side of the man is seen when you visit his tomb. Buried right next to him is a servant, his faithful valet. If you study the history of the times, you will find that that humble servant was married in the great mansion of the Hermitage. You will find that Jackson, in his will, gave him a lifetime position. All his life, he lived next to Jackson and is buried beside him. When you consider the social inequities of that time, you see an amazing bond between master and servant, between a President and his valet.

Prince Philip is known everywhere as the handsome husband of Queen Elizabeth II of Great Britain. He was born a prince of Greece, though no Greek blood flows through his veins. He is, instead, of German and Danish ancestry. As a baby, he was smuggled out of Greece in a crate made from an orange box. That hardly befits a prince! Later, he took the last name of his English uncle, Mountbatten. Now he is known as the consort of his wife, Queen Elizabeth II. You talk about an identity problem! We all have identity problems. We have spiritual identity problems. Revelation, chapter one, says God has made us kings and priests, yet the Gospels and the epistles say we are servants and slaves. We are paupers who are heirs of the world! We are peasants who shall someday rule the world!

Few pictures are more quickly recognized than the picture of that magnificent Swiss mountain, the Matterhorn. The classic view is taken from Zermatt, a small Alpine village. That classic view can be seen only from the steps of the church in Zermatt! So the church gives us the best viewpoint of life, the clearest picture of who we are and what we are meant to be.

Darius, with his Persian Empire, was threatened by the conquering armies of Alexander the Great. He offered a truce. He offered to give Alexander one third of his empire, his daughter in marriage, and three hundred million dollars! Alexander's trusted adviser, Parmenion, said, "Were I Alexander, I would accept." Said Alexander, "So would I, were I Parmenion," and he refused. Our decisions are governed by our sense of identity. Do you know what and who you are?

We do not understand the slavery of the New Testament. We see it only in terms of *Uncle Tom's Cabin.* It was a different kind of bondage. It was more economic than physical. Slaves were often teachers and thinkers. In many cities, the most educated people in town were slaves. To understand this helps us to see how Paul could urge Onesimus to go back into slavery under Philemon. Paul could accept the economic order of his day if it were leavened by the spirit and influence of Christian love. And always, Paul saw in the economic order an illustration of the spiritual order of things—Christ our Master, we His willing subjects and bond servants.

Textbooks
by Standard Publishing:

The Christian Minister
  Sam E. Stone
Introduction to Christian Education
  Eleanor Daniel, John W. Wade, Charles Gresham
Ministering to Youth
  David Roadcup, editor
The Church on Purpose
  Joe Ellis

Commentary on Acts
  J. W. McGarvey
The Equipping Ministry
  Paul Benjamin
Essays on New Testament Christianity
  C. Robert Wetzel, editor
The Fourfold Gospel
  J. W. McGarvey and P. Y. Pendleton
The Jesus Years
  Thomas D. Thurman
How to Understand the Bible
  Knofel Staton
Teach With Success
  Guy P. Leavitt, revised by Eleanor Daniel
God's Plan for Church Leadership
  Knofel Staton

Available at your Christian bookstore or

STANDARD
PUBLISHING